The Way of Reckoning
by
Joyce Collins

© 2020 Truthteller Publishing™

www.truthtellerpub.com

All rights reserved
3rd Edition, 1st Printing February 2020
ISBN 978-0-9743024-3-0

Cover by Johnny Dallahan
Illustrations by Joyce Collins

Foreword

I am an incest survivor. In previous editions, I stated that my father first raped me when I was six years old and continued well into my adolescence. I now know the abuse began before I could speak. My psyche coped with that trauma by splitting in two—a child who experienced every moment of the abuse and another child who knew nothing of it. In her book, *Miss America by Day*, Marilyn Van Derbur, also an incest survivor, calls these personas the night child and day child. Neither my night child nor day child knew the other existed until my repressed memories surfaced at the age of 37—some 20 years after the abuse ended.

I have been writing poetry since I was 15, most of it sad, much of it philosophical—all of it insightful even though I didn't yet have the ability to understand the insight. In retrospect, it is as if I were writing for a future me whose task was to re-integrate my night child and day child into a whole person. The title of this book, *The Way of Reckoning,* is the title of the first poem I wrote after my memories surfaced. It is the quintessential example of a poem written for the future me, describing both the violent upheaval I was beginning and the revelation of truth that would result.

If you are a sexual abuse survivor, I hope this book helps you. I hope the poems give words to the feelings you haven't been able to express. I hope the poems let you know you are not alone in having these feelings. Lastly, I hope this book gives you hope that your wounds will heal as mine have. If you have not experienced sexual abuse, I offer this book as insight into the mind and soul of someone who has walked that path and come out on the other side.

Acknowledgements

I want to thank my sister, who has passed since I published the previous edition, for believing me. I want to thank my mother for being my rock through all the remembering. I also want to thank my therapist, Susan Hartman, for guiding me on this journey and my psychiatrist, Luz Stark, for prescribing me medications that saved me from taking my own life. Lastly, I want to thank Marilyn Van Derbur for writing her book. It was a lifeline to hope that healing was possible.

How to Find a Poem

About half of my poems are titled. The others are numbered, and I list them in the Table of Contents with the first line of the poem.

Table of Contents

Titled Poems 1
    The Way of Reckoning 2
    Letting Go 4
    Paradigm 4
    Rage 4
    Sharing Tree 5
    The Soul 5
    Haunted 6
    Depression 6
    Fear 7
    Gut Wound 7
    Addiction 8
    Outcome 8
    A Penny of Grace 9
    Deaf Until I Listen 9
    The One 10
    Plea 10
    Enough 11
    Sin-Sick Soul 12
    Ode to Inigo Montoya 13
    Peace 14
    A Bit of Space 15
    Insight 15

Bridges 16
Obligated 16
Once 17
Safe Space 17
Powerlessness 17
Survivor Tilt 18
Too Much Day 18
Transformation 18
Marriage Vows 18
Life-ful Place 19
Flashback 19
Go Yearning 20
Arms Around Shoulders 20
Why I Pick at Bumps on My Skin 21
Sit With It 21
Remember to… 22

Numbered Poems 24
Time served two the gem of joy 25
Belittle, belittle, belittle 25
Life is not a closet 25
What a place this silence is— 26
Anger to pain is preferable— 26
Such delight I find in him. 27

Silence is action	27
resting place	27
Sometimes I thrash	28
God lays his quilt across the trees	29
Truth is price and purchase,	29
Healing is an iterative process,	30
Two rocks lie on either side of a path	30
I shall send Reality to burn at your side	30
Alone in the desert	31
When my mother wore rose-colored glasses,	31
I long for the world where souls mate for life	31
I never thought to live in my house,	32
We walk the fence of self-esteem,	32
Every deed both cruel and kind	33
Childhood is when we get our wounds	33
I feel sorry for the house—	34
My Father taught me plenty	35
On the anniversary of my death	36
The insects swarm over me,	37
I am not who I've been,	38

Titled Poems

The Way of Reckoning

Reptiles drop their tails in fright
and live to grow another.
Humans split the limb alike,
but bind it with a tether,
so long and thin as time goes by,
we think of it as other.

But memory grows its tendrils out
from wounded limb to well,
and bides its time 'til boundary thins
and tendrils' touch is felt.

Then all hell breaks loose—
or that's the way it seems
as tendrils hook, then pull apart
the self I know as me.

A foulness spills out my bowels
and takes my life-force with it.
Where food once fed is nauseous dread.
My stomach yields its content.

My head is wracked with migraine pain
and fear is strong for madness.
All these confuse and mis'ry bring,
but none compare the sadness.

Illness say doctors—Nay!
I know the past is beckoning.
I am not sick from bug or germ.
It is the way of reckoning—

to tell the tale and tell it whole,
each unto the other, until they realize
they are we and we are the survivor.

Letting Go

To cling to what I treasure,
and shun what I fear,
is not in itself the vice.
That lies within the blind I wear,
and the will to pay its price—

To never know the value
in the consequence I fear,
Or the detriment to life itself
of that which I hold dear

Paradigm

$$\text{Probability} = \frac{\text{Fear}}{\text{Want}}$$

Rage

I feel the strength in my arms
shooting out my fists
Pummeling, Pummeling, Pummeling
until exhaustion relinquishes my mind
back to reason
My eyes open and I see
what I have done

Sharing Tree

The Giving Tree I thought was good
Now I see unhealthy wood
It gave of self in rarest form,
yet reaped no love in return
It gave and gave 'til none was left,
save a stump—its one last gift
And still the boy does not see
the value of the Giving Tree
So when comes the very last page,
The boy is tired and worn with age
Despite the tree's steadfast will,
the boy is old and unhappy still
I wonder would things different be
If it had been a sharing tree

The Soul

The soul is like a sphere whose radius extends
not in one direction, but all
Bursting forth in equal proportion,
a great ball of light

Though dressed in honor, she wears no airs,
For she sees with equal clarity
Life's majesty and absurdity—
Calling at once for both humble reverence
and hysterical laughter

Haunted

By the memories
of what I saw
of what I did
of what I did nothing about
of guilt
of shame
of horrible, horrible helplessness
hers
and mine

Depression

Like a knock on a door
I cannot refuse to answer
It arrives, and I dread its coming—
its weight
For there's no carrying this load,
Only bearing it—
Upright
Then falling to my knees,
'til finally prostrate
And still it stays and weighs
heavy on my back
Then goes, unannounced—
Quietly,
As it came

Fear

I carry it—
like luggage
It is heavy and a burden
But I need it I think,
lest I cast my lot completely—
in favor of joy

Gut Wound

A dream dies—mortally wounded
by the acceptance of reality
I ask it to go quietly
but it does not
It is a gut wound

I cry out to God,
"Why are you? Why do you?"
Do this to me
But no answer comes

After a time, I alter my question.
"How do I find it?"
"In what form comes relief?"
Soon comes the answer,
In grief
In grief

Addiction

Come on down!
Try your luck!
You know it's bound to change
The past is past
Don't look back.
You have so much to gain

The game's the same
You know it well
By now you are the best
Just pick the time, the place, the face.
I will do the rest

I guarantee consistency
This game will end the same—
Time and time again
This game will end the same you see—
Just for you my friend

Outcome

Why is it so, the less that I know,
the more certain I am of its content?

Fearful thinking fills the void
because the unknown is infinite

A Penny of Grace

I went to the prayer box,
my soul hungry and nude
And found a penny of grace
for shelter and food

A penny of grace—
all I required,
had been left in the box
by someone inspired

When I returned,
I dropped in a dime
For a needier soul
at a needier time

Deaf Until I Listen

I try to make her see it—
this wounded child of mine
Nothing is as it was
There's no reason for the pain,
but she is deaf until I listen,
rigid until I yield, all—
consuming until I surrender,
lame until I bridge the gap
and walk it back again

The One

I see your face at the end of wait,
the one day of someday,
the liquid of longing gone past

It is to me the fulfillment of dreams,
the soothing of wounds,
the rising of joy at last

All this would be so
I know, I know
If your lot with mine
were cast

Plea

Have mercy, Lord, Let me go
Have mercy, Lord, Compassion show

Spare me from this vicious cure
Not one more scream can I endure

Let me die as six or eight
It hurts too much to integrate

Enough

Enough he would say
when he didn't want to play anymore

Enough tennis…
(You hit the ball over the fence too many times)

Enough frisbee…
(You made too many bad throws)

Enough wrestling…
(You're starting to win)

Enough spending time with you
(That I really didn't want to do)

Enough bearing the terrible burden
of your longing to be with mé

Enough it should be to fulfill my obligation

But it was never enough and the words
in parentheses always tainted time he gave,

Always dashed the illusion that I was special
at all, much less enough to inspire his love

Sin-Sick Soul

Sometimes whisper, Sometimes shout
Always fear, Always doubt
This voice inside I can't block out

To the world I show a face
Of confidence, Of poise and grace
These things are real, But only part
What's in my soul, What's in my heart

If I don't edit, They'll find out
Confirm my shame and my doubt
Once again I'll hide my face
I'll be put back
in my place

Who am I to ask so much?
For love, affection, Human touch
To happiness I have no right
Cease my song—Put out my light

Who I am is an offense
Is the message I receive
Despite opposing evidence,
That's the message I believe

Ode to Inigo Montoya

Hello, my name is memory
You raped your daughter,
who loved you dearly
I do not lie

Hello, my name is will
On her you imposed me,
while you drank your fill.
It drained her dry

Hello, my name is shame
I served you well
Wracked is she with guilt and blame,
but ne'er you cry

Hello, my name is terror
With me you broke her mind
Day and night, I pursued her
Nameless and faceless was I

Hello, my name is rage
I was that daughter
Now I am not her
Prepare to die

Peace

There is no hurry
There is no wait
There is no early
There is no late

I no longer seek distraction
from ever-present anxiety
There's no discomfort in the now—
It's not prickly like it used to be

I've no concern for the future
The past no longer drives me
Instead I float—as on a raft,
And let the river guide me

My soul rejoices in this freedom
I breathe so ever easily
I know now that I belong
to a god who loves me dotingly

A Bit of Space

There's a bit of space
'tween the pieces of me
that leads me to compartmentalize
and mask incongruity
that I might otherwise realize
if I had the whole scenery

Insight

Thank you, Humiliation
You were my teacher

Thank you, Compassion
You were my lesson

Thank you, Circumstance
You were my keeper

Thank you, Consequence
You were my pen

Thank you, Disillusionment
You showed me I was blind

Thank you, Blindness
You eased the way

Bridges

It was not until I reached
the second bridge
that I truly realized
I'd crossed the first

It was not until I crossed
the second bridge
that I could not deny
the many more

Obligated

to feel what I don't
to act like I do
to give without receiving
because of who I am to you
to comfort when I am grieving
when I don't know what to do
to agonize over the desire to cut ties
and be done,
to cut ties and move on
to try to make you happy
to do what I think I should
to be a good person
to do what a good person would

Once

Once, I thought if I saw him,
I would see that he was not he,
And I was not she
But now I know I would not—
For once when I saw him,
although it was not him,
I froze right there on the spot

Safe Space

I need a space where she has not invaded—
where what is happening is not happening
has not happened
will not happen
is not even in the equation
A place where I live alone
as one of three and fear and sadness
do not dance with me

Powerlessness

There are no tears for the crying inside,
no screams for the too terrified
no blows for rage trapped in mind prisons, and
no trip back in time
to turn tables on these visions

Survivor Tilt

When I feel now as I did then,
I but one-way bend —
It is now, as I knew it would
happening again

Too Much Day

When I'm depressed and I sleep,
I pray the Lord my soul to keep
And when I early wake, I pray
Go back to sleep—
too much day

Transformation

Avoid, avoid, avoid
Defend, defend
Reach, grasp, enjoy
Then enjoy again

Marriage Vows

To have and to hold
for better, for worse
for richer, for poorer
in sickness, in health
'til death do us part
I pledge myself to You —
my lawful wedded Life

Life-ful Place

I find I want to kill what I am afraid to embrace—
whether it be spiders, roaches, or male sexuality

Now I am called to see them not as monsters,
but as love with a new face

This thought once impossible, has become but improbable—
that everything contained in life has a
life-ful place

Flashback

My stomach lives in fear of food,
so I chew without tasting
and swallow through the side of my mouth

I tap my hands on my legs,
picture safe faces,
and say, "This is not happening now"

Go Yearning

We are only shadows of ourselves
until we know the hell we've been through

Yearning plumbs the depths of true

Go yearning, Go yearning
Go rise, Go tell

Go yearning, Go yearning
Go rise, Go tell

Arms Around Shoulders

I make things happen,
I get things done—
My will moves mountains
But you, you call me to give comfort in a crisis
When anger moves me to make things happen,
You model compassionate presence
You inspire me to wrap arms around shoulders
for the duration of the journey
And let others repave the road

Why I Pick at Bumps on My Skin

Because it is there—
Because it is not smooth—
Because it is rough—
Because it resists me—
Because it is not of me—
Because it is in me—
Because it has a root
and the root is in me
I have to get it out
I have to get it out
I have to get it OUT

And finally, I do
And I feel relief…

And release

And the blood flows
And I am free again

Sit With It

I sit quietly and cry at least
two streams from closed lids

glad to ignore the alarm on my phone
glad to sit with it—alone

Remember to...

buy that thing
send that package
take out the trash
take out the recycle
close the windows
do laundry
check the mail
mail the check
floss and brush
take your meds
refill your meds
pick up your meds
make that call
send that text
send that e-mail
return that call
reply to that text
reply to that e-mail
make that appointment
put that appointment on your calendar
set a reminder for that appointment
prepare for that appointment
put that on your To Do list
look at your To Do list

Remember to... remember YOU

take that shower
get that rest
eat good food
spend time with yourself

spend time on yourself
reconnect with the universe
move your body
write poetry
and breathe

Numbered Poems

~ 1 ~

Time served two the gem of joy
each on mirrored plate
One did hurry to capture the prize;
the other thought to wait
Death saw naught but refracted light,
and at his plate did hiss
Life, instead, cast aside the rock
and gazed into the face of bliss

~ 2 ~

Belittle, belittle, belittle
Become undone, be naught
Be little, be little, be little
Become, by one, be taught

~ 3 ~

Life is not a closet
from which we may choose an
emotion, disposition, or perspective
It is more like a nanny,
who chooses from her own closet
what we shall wear that day

~ 4 ~

What a place this silence is—
I think I like it here
There's nothing to remind me—
No consequence to fear

I can almost say and do and be
all my heart desires
And never face the certainty
that action soon requires

I can walk the earth and never move
a single grain of sand
What a place this silence is—
This almost living land

Yes, I think I like it here—
I'm never going back.
Look! A tree to rest my bones
I think I'll take a nap

~ 5 ~

Anger to pain is preferable—
Numbness better still
Best of all, to bind them all,
and sugar coat the pill

~ 6 ~

Such delight I find in him.
In him my mate I see
My soul is filled with longing
For words from silence free
Alas, I'm trapped—
he wears a ring
His door is closed to me

~ 7 ~

Silence is action
loud as words
what deafens the ear
cannot be heard

~ 8 ~

resting place
moving place
open place
my heart

~ 9 ~

Sometimes I thrash
with bitter stroke
in a pool of discontent
And then, my anger spent,
I dry myself on a rock of sadness
under a sky that has no sun
I do these things
and let them claim me
for they and I are one

~ 10 ~

God lays his quilt across the trees
and paints the ground with its leaves
Each bears the color of its fruit,
some flamboyant—others mute

Orange orange and lemon yellow,
ruby red and golden mellow,
McIntosh with pumpkin patch,
deep plum pudding and a dash—
pistachio

And though my eyes can't drink their fill,
the season offers greater still
Such sweet aroma fills my breath
to wake my primal union with my
soul and senses one and all
I love thee, love thee, love thee, Fall!

~ 11 ~

Truth is price and purchase,
burden and relief,
and Passage from endless fear
to finite joy and grief

~ 12 ~

Healing is an iterative process,
a progressive probing hex
The first step is agony, followed by a rest
Successive steps improve by the delta
Agony—x

~ 13 ~

Two rocks lie on either side of a path
They are mates—
their faces tell me so,
"We were one, but now are two—
cleaved by brutal blow"

I notice as I pass between,
a faint ambillic flow
It is, I think, their former wholeness
refusing to let go

~ 14 ~

I shall send Reality to burn at your side
and illuminate the face of Illusion

~ 15 ~

Alone in the desert
I long to be free and scream out the pain
But when I think of it,
I hold myself in
The burning sensation
will only get worse if I let myself feel it—
the depth of my thirst

~ 16 ~

When my mother wore rose-colored glasses,
the world was always fine
And if it wasn't really that way,
It'd surely be in time
But then one day she took them off—
much to my surprise
But even more the shock
when I did come to find
She'd worn the lens for many eyes,
and one of them was mine

~ 17 ~

I long for the world where souls mate for life
and breathe unmitigated truth.
Whose speech is unfettered by faces that lie
And life is not jaded by fear

~ 18 ~

I never thought to live in my house,
to renovate the rooms
I only sought to get out
To live in something new

Ten times I left
Ten times I built
that house again the same
from breakfast nook to ceiling fan
from brick to window pane

In my rage, I tore it down—
stripped it to the frame,
and in the end, found myself out
through a door that opened in

~ 19 ~

We walk the fence of self-esteem,
our faces toward the sun,
but never leaping there
It's all we can do—
keep our feet on the beam,
And avoid the shadow's lair

~ 20 ~

Every deed both cruel and kind
falls on fertile ground
and finds a mate to spawn again
'til kings of kings are crowned

Tempt this does to measure worth
of praise or scarlet letter—
tally thorn and vine since birth
and sum the deeds together

But all our deeds are potter's clay
at last if not at first
None can take our worth away
or nullify our worst

~ 21 ~

Childhood is when we get our wounds
Adulthood is when we feel them
And if we persevere,
It is when we heal them

~ 22 ~

I feel sorry for the house—
for the walls that had to hide,
to hold, to hold inside
for the wallpaper
stuck there, trapped there
with eyes that wouldn't close,
for the roof that had to keep it together,
make it all seem sound,
for the floor on which I hid by my bed,
that small space I controlled
It had to know. It had to know.
I feel sorry for the house

My Father taught me plenty
Although he doesn't know it
He taught myself to hate me
To love, but not to show it

My father taught me distance
And the judgement it implies
He taught me to fear weakness
And the consequence it buys

My father taught me doing
To from my feelings hide
It is from him I'm fleeing
Though he has long since died

~ 24 ~

On the anniversary of my death
I remember pain
Such as I had never known before
Such as I had never known possible
I remember betrayal
Such as I had never known at all
I remember my soul consumed by fire
Not yet a phoenix, but ashes

I remember this anniversary
Inconceivable and unwanted—
loathed even
At the time
All this returns to me
All this is in the present
All this is in the past
On the anniversary of my death

~ 25 ~

The insects swarm over me,
biting and stinging and sucking my skin
I clamp myself tight,
but they force their way in
My nerves are all screaming,
but I dare not cry
If I feel what I'm feeling, I know I will die
The insects are incest,
but they can't be responsible
Like bees with a flower,
they just do what comes natural
When they finally go,
when they got what they came for
My position is fetal, curled on the floor
My mind has exploded;
my psyche is shattered
Could he have known,
and would it have mattered?
The insects are incest;
it's too much to endure
I know that tomorrow
they'll come back for more

~ 26 ~

I am not who I've been,
the person you know
I've been a shadow—
A ghost in a show

The color of appropriate
The tune of just-right
The shape of fits-in
The line of in-sight

Now I am nova—
brilliantly bright,
life-changing color,
sight-seeking light

My moments are chock-full—
the realest of real
I think what I think
I feel what I feel

Sometimes I look back
at how I was then,
the lessons I re-learned
again and again.

Those rules I created
had hemmed me in
Thanks to the tearing,
I'm not who I've been

www.ingramcontent.com/pod-product-compliance
Lightning Source LLC
Chambersburg PA
CBHW051712090426
42736CB00013B/2671